CHAR

CHARGE TO VICTORY
The Story of Oliver Cromwell

By Annabel Brunner

Illustrated by Edward Blake

ANGLIA *young* BOOKS

First published in 1990
by Anglia Young Books
Durhams Farmhouse, Ickleton
Saffron Walden, Essex CB10 1SR

Illustrations by Edward Blake

British Library Cataloguing in Publication Data
Brunner, Annabel
    Charge to victory: the story of Oliver Cromwell.
    1. England. Cromwell, Oliver
    I. Title
    942.004

    ISBN 1–871173–09–4

Typeset in Palatino
and printed in Great Britain by
Redwood Press Limited, Melksham, Wiltshire

AUTHOR'S NOTE

Oliver Cromwell has the reputation, for many people, of having been a puritanical dictatorial man. However, as I researched his life it became clear to me that this reputation was ill deserved. Cromwell was, in fact, a typical family man of his era, albeit one with strong views and the determination to do what he felt was right. Like many others in those troubled times he was caught up in a war which set brother against brother and which resulted in the execution of the king. Cromwell was probably the most brilliant cavalryman of his day and laid the basis for the first standing army that existed in England. However, he was not simply a man of war and his involvement in Parliament also had a significant effect on its later development into the democratic body that it is today. As a young man he was something of a rebel and like many such young men his attitudes changed dramatically as he grew to full adulthood after his father died and he became responsible for his family's well being. To remember him as a traitor is to view him from only the narrowest of angles as he was a complex and persuasive man whose concern was for the well being of many less fortunate than himself.

The complex historical background and political events have been simplified and in some places I have imagined what Cromwell and other characters might have said.

I am very grateful for the help provided by Richard Young at Huntingdon Library.

I became an admirer of 'Our Chief of Men'. I hope you do too.

CHAPTER ONE

HINCHINGBROOKE 1603

'Come on, Oliver. We are going to miss the presents. Uncle Oliver is about to give them to the king.' Clutching half-eaten sweetmeats in their hands, Oliver and his elder brother, Henry, ran through the crowd, ducking between the velvet breeches and silk dresses, pausing only to wipe their sticky fingers on the back of a red dress. Luckily the lady wearing it was so busy looking at the king that she did not notice. At last they were in a position to see clearly and Oliver stared in wonder at the presents of horses, hounds, hawks and a magnificent cup of gold.

It was the first time that he had seen a king and although he was only four years old, he was not very impressed. He thought that the new king of England should be tall and golden, but King James was short and dark and had bandy legs. Also he spoke with a thick Scots accent so Oliver couldn't understand a word he said.

Oliver and his family were spending a few days at Hinchingbrooke House on the outskirts of Huntingdon. Queen Elizabeth had died without leaving any children. Her heir was her second cousin, James VI of Scotland and now King James was travelling down to London to be crowned James I of England. As he and his courtiers made their way south, they were being entertained by landowners who were keen to make a good impression on their new sovereign. One of these landowners was Oliver's uncle, Sir Oliver Cromwell, the owner of Hinchingbrooke House.

This beautiful house had been given to the Cromwell family many years ago. Oliver's grandfather, Sir Henry Cromwell, had been knighted by Queen Elizabeth. He had turned the old nunnery into a house and had built extensions from the newest material, red bricks.

Grandfather Henry had been a very important person in the Huntingdon area. He had been a sheriff for Cambridge and a Member of Parliament (MP) for Huntingdon. He was known locally as the 'Golden Knight'. This was a very suitable nickname for him because he had spent a lot of money entertaining Queen Elizabeth at Hinchingbrooke and he used to ride through the villages, throwing gold coins from his coach to the poor people.

Sir Oliver Cromwell, who was Oliver's godfather as well as his uncle was the eldest son of the 'Golden Knight'. He had inherited Hinchingbrooke House and he was determined to give the new king a good time. He had even had a new bow window built onto his dining room in honour of the visit.

Oliver looked at the king again. He certainly seemed to be enjoying himself. There had been feasts with delicious food and good wine and entertainments. Important guests had come from all over Cambridgeshire to meet their new monarch. Oliver was sure that King James was pleased with his welcome. He put his arm on Uncle Oliver's shoulder and said 'Well, mon, you've treated me better than anyone since I left Edinburgh.' Uncle Oliver seemed very happy at these words. It was obviously important to make a good impression on the new king.

After the king had left Hinchingbrooke, Oliver and his family rode back to their own home in the centre of Huntingdon, a short distance away. Oliver's father, Robert Cromwell, was the second son of the 'Golden Knight'. His father had bought him a house and some farming land in Huntingdon. Oliver's father was a quiet, gentle man who was not as important as his elder brother, but he was well thought of in Huntingdon.

As they covered the half mile between Hinchingbrooke and the centre of Huntingdon, Robert Cromwell looked across at the carriage in which the rest of his family was travelling. He smiled to himself. For once Oliver was sitting quietly and not bouncing around.

'Did you enjoy seeing your new king, Oliver? It's not many boys who get a chance to see a king so close.' But Oliver did not reply. Full of sweetmeats and worn out after the day's festivities, his eyes had closed and he was fast asleep, his head resting against Henry's shoulder.

CHAPTER TWO

EARLY DAYS IN HUNTINGDON

When Oliver was a youngster, Huntingdon was not much more than a large village on the north bank of the River Ouse. The arched stone bridge crossed the river at the southern end of the village and the Cromwell house was at the northern end of the main street, not far from St. John's Church where Oliver had been christened. It was a big house with plenty of rooms for a large family and a few servants. Oliver was born in 1599. He was the fifth child in the family. His parents were to have five more children, but as was usual in those days, not all of them lived to become adults. Although Oliver was one of three sons, he was the only one to survive childhood.

The house was built on the site of an Augustinian friary and some of the old stone walls remained as part of the building. Near the house was the brick conduit which brought fresh water into Huntingdon and beyond that stretched the farmland which was owned by Oliver's father. It was only a few minutes walk to the George Inn and All Hallows Church. Oliver particularly enjoyed going to the market place which was always busy. He liked wandering among the 'leanetoos' looking at the produce which was for sale.

Oliver's childhood was happy. His father was a gentle man who enjoyed spending time with his young son. His mother kept a good house and still had time to have fun with her many children. Oliver loved horses and became an excellent rider at an early age. He played in the street with other children, fished in the river and streams and best of all, he rode out with his father to inspect his farmland and other properties.

To begin with he was taught reading and writing by his mother and a governess. He then had a tutor called Mr Long, but at the age of seven the first big change took place in his life. He went to school.

The Free School was only a few minutes walk from his house. Oliver felt quite nervous as he walked down the street on his first day. He had heard that Dr Beard, the master, was very strict and shouted a lot. When he walked into the one room which was the only classroom, he felt even more nervous. All the other boys were sitting in silence and they watched him as he walked to his place.

'Ah, young Oliver,' boomed the tall figure dressed in black. 'Welcome! In this school, we work hard and follow the path that God has set for us.' Oliver felt rather like a little brown sparrow in the shadow of a big, black rook.

However, things were not was bad as he thought. Although Dr Beard was a fiery preacher who shouted his message about God from the pulpit, he was a kind, sympathetic teacher. He became a close friend of the family and was even asked to be a witness to Robert Cromwell's will.

Oliver learnt arithmetic, geometry, Latin and history. He spent a lot of time studying the Bible, learning psalms and reading sermons. He found the Bible quite an exciting book – there were some vivid descriptions of exciting battles and sieges, if you knew where to look.

Like Dr Beard and many other families in the area, the Cromwells were Puritans. This meant that they preferred churches which were simply furnished, without ornaments and decorations. They liked their priests to be dressed in plain robes and their services to be straightforward, without too much singing and ceremony. Most of all, they enjoyed a good stirring sermon. Oliver was taught that it was important to be honest, to work hard, to do what you believed to be right, guided by your faith in God.

It was very exciting listening to Dr Beard preach. Oliver certainly didn't fall asleep when he was speaking.

'The wicked will be punished in this life as well as the next,' he would boom. 'Kings and princes are also subject to God's justice. They cannot escape the consequences of their actions. God will revenge himself on those who break his laws. He will choose those who will carry out his tasks on this earth.'

Oliver was very impressed by these stirring words. Dr Beard had a great influence on him. They were to remain in touch long after Oliver had left his school. His teachings were to stay with him throughout his life.

Oliver was no scholar. He preferred to play football and to wrestle with boys of his own age. He loved going out into the fens which surrounded the fields around his house. It was a secret world full of wild duck and geese, fish and reeds. As he grew older he became skilled at shooting the longbow and hawking and hunting.

He was not a particularly well-behaved boy, in fact he could be very naughty. He crept over orchard walls and stole apples, he raided dovecotes and took the plump birds, he broke down hedges and he played truant from school. Many were the times that he came home covered in mud or wet from a ducking in the stream and many were the beatings that he had from his father and from Dr Beard. He had a quick temper and could be very stubborn. He was also a loner who could be moody when things did not go his way. On the other hand, he was very affectionate and would always stick up for the underdog and protect those who he felt had been treated unfairly.

The years passed and at the age of seventeen, he was

ready to leave Huntingdon and travel fifteen miles south to the City of Cambridge.

On 23rd April, 1616, the day Shakespeare died, Oliver entered Sidney Sussex College as a Fellow Commoner.

CHAPTER THREE

HEAD OF THE FAMILY

Sidney Sussex College was a new College. It had only been in existence for some eighteen years. Its Master was a Puritan called Dr Samuel Ward who was very strict. Oliver and another student shared a room which looked out onto Sidney Street. Oliver thoroughly enjoyed his student life in Cambridge. Once again, he showed that he was not an outstanding student. He was fond of music, quite good at maths and geography and enjoyed reading history, but academic life did not come easily to him and he had to work hard at his studies.

Although he did not do a lot of reading, he was very impressed by one book. This was called 'History of the World', written by Sir Walter Raleigh. In this book Raleigh tried to show that bad kings were punished by God. Naturally enough, King James was not impressed by this book, which became a best-seller, and he tried to have it banned.

There were very strict rules at Sidney Sussex and students could be fined or whipped if they broke them. They were not allowed to gamble, go bull or bear baiting or visit taverns. Oliver was not a model student and he probably disobeyed these rules on many occasions. He was certainly well-known as an athlete, showing himself to be a talented football player and skilled with the cudgels.

After he had been there about a year, he was sitting in his room one day, reading quietly. He had some work to make up as he had just returned from Huntingdon where there had been a family celebration. His older sister, Margaret, had married Valentine Walton, the son of a neighbouring squire. There was a knock at the door. A fellow student came in bringing a message which had just arrived from home.

'What is the matter?' he said, for Oliver had read the message and had then sat still, his face white. When Oliver did not reply, he picked up the message and read it for himself.

'Come on, Oliver,' he said sympathetically. 'Show me where your belongings are, I will help you pack, for you must return home at once.'

●●●●●

Oliver returned home. His father had died, suddenly and very unexpectedly. Oliver's elder brother, Henry, was already dead so Oliver was now the head of a large family. He had a mother and five sisters to look after. His youngest sister was still only six. His duty was clear, he must leave university and run the farm.

Oliver did not find it difficult to look after his inheritance. His father had taught him well. What he had not realised was how much he would miss his father. For many months he felt a great sadness and the responsibilities he had taken on weighed heavily on his young shoulders. His missed his father's guiding hand and advice.

For a short while, Oliver tried to find comfort by having a

good time when he was not working. He gambled, drank and borrowed money. In general he made a nuisance of himself and some of the practical jokes he played on friends and relations were not well received.

He became very close to his mother and she understood him well. She realised that he needed a change and so it was agreed that she would run the farm for a while and Oliver would go to London, to Lincoln's Inn, to study law as his father, grandfather and two of his uncles had done before him.

It was a wise decision. Oliver enjoyed life in London. He had to work hard, but he still found time to look up his cousin, John Hampden and to make new friends.

One of these new friends was Sir James Bourchier who was a wealthy fur dealer and leather dresser and had six children. Oliver spent time at the Bourchier's London house and at their country home in Essex. The eldest daughter, Elizabeth, was a pretty, rather plump girl with a good sense of humour. She fell in love with the sturdy country squire from Huntingdon. On 22nd May, 1620, Elizabeth and Oliver were married in St Giles' Church, Cripplegate, in London.

It was a good match. Oliver was not handsome but he was attractive in a rugged way. His nose was rather large, but his eyes were his best feature. They were green-grey, heavy lidded and gentle. He wore his brown hair quite long as was the fashion in those days. He had a strong personality and he could get very angry, but he was also thoughtful and gentle. He was not a man to be ignored.

It was to be a very happy marriage. Elizabeth was devoted to her husband. They had nine children and their letters to each other over the years show that they loved each other throughout their long married life.

They returned to the house in Huntingdon together and Elizabeth quickly fitted in with the rest of the family. It was a happy time. Oliver was kept busy on the farm and Elizabeth had many household tasks, but there was still time for picnics and for Oliver's favourite pastimes – hunting and hawking. The family grew quickly and by the time the King summoned a new Parliament in 1628, Oliver and Elizabeth had five children.

Once again, Oliver set off for London, but this time as one of the two newly elected Members of Parliament for Huntingdon.

As a member of a well-known local family with a number of close relations who were also in Parliament, Oliver was an obvious choice to represent Huntingdon in the House of Commons.

Sadly, Hinchingbrooke House no longer belonged to the family. It had been sold to the Earl of Manchester. Oliver's uncle had entertained King James so well that he had made many more visits, no doubt expecting even more expensive presents. Uncle Oliver had run out of money!

CHAPTER FOUR

EARLY DAYS IN PARLIAMENT

James I had died in 1625 and his son had become King Charles I. From the start of his reign, Charles and Parliament had quarrelled. Charles believed that he had been appointed by God to rule and that Parliament was there to obey his commands. Parliament felt that it should have some say in how Charles ran the country. Charles resented Parliament's interference and neither side trusted the other. This state of affairs was to continue for many years with Charles and his Parliament moving further and further down the path to Civil War.

The House of Commons in 1628 was an exciting place. Charles had summoned Parliament because he needed money. Parliament wouldn't give him any until he had agreed to their demands which they had set out in a 'Petition of Right'. Charles had to accept this Petition and bonfires were lit in the street to celebrate, but the people quickly learnt that Charles had no intention of keeping his promises.

Parliament was also very unhappy about the changes Charles and his religious adviser, Bishop Laud, were making to religious services. They were afraid that England might become a Catholic country again, particularly since the Queen was a Catholic and had a lot of influence over her husband. There were many religious debates which became very heated.

'No Popery!' shouted both Parliament and the country. Oliver himself took part in one of these debates and spoke in the House of Commons for the first time.

Charles decided to adjourn Parliament, but the members would not let him until they had finished a very important debate. Several MP's held the Speaker down in his chair until they had finished. Needless to say, Charles was furious. He dismissed Parliament, imprisoned some of the MPs and decided to rule the country without them.

Parliament was not to meet again for eleven years.

Oliver returned home to Huntingdon. It wasn't long before he got involved in a local argument about the town's new Charter. He felt that the ordinary people were being treated unfairly and he said so in no uncertain terms. He was so rude about the new Mayor that he was summoned to London and asked to explain 'his disgraceful and unseemly speeches.'

Oliver had to apologise. He had spoken 'in heat and passion'. However, he still felt that the rights of the people of Huntingdon were being ignored and his point was taken up. The Mayor and Aldermen of Huntingdon were ordered to make sure that the people of the town were not treated unjustly.

Unfortunately, life did not go smoothly for Oliver over the next few years. The farm was not doing well. The harvests were poor and money was short. Oliver sold his property in Huntingdon for £1800 and moved with his family to St.Ives.

There he lived quietly as a farmer on a rented property.

Life was peaceful. His sheep were sent to market with the O.C. brand on their backs and he and his family went regularly to the local church. He watched his children grow up. It was a time to reflect and think. Meanwhile storm clouds were fast building up over the whole country.

CHAPTER FIVE

A MOVE TO ELY

In 1636, Oliver's fortunes changed. Sir Thomas Steward, his uncle on his mother's side died and left his estate in Ely to Oliver.

The family moved into the attractive half-timbered house which was a short walk across the Palace Green to the magnificent cathedral. Money became easier, the younger children went to school in Ely and the two eldest boys went to boarding school in Felsted.

It wasn't long before Oliver was fighting for the under-dog again. This time the row was over the draining of the fens. Oliver had accepted that it was a good idea and that the whole district would benefit from the reclaimed land. After all, both his father and uncle had been involved in similar schemes. However, as work started, he quickly realised that the fenmen who made their living from the fens, were getting a raw deal. They would lose their public rights such as grazing, fishing and fowling and other people would take all the profits. There were riots. Oliver promised the fenmen that he would defend them, in court if necessary. He became their spokesman. The Crown agreed that the public rights should continue for the time being and Oliver was nicknamed 'Lord of the Fens'.

Oliver's joy at this local victory didn't last long. Heart-breaking news arrived from Felsted. His eldest son, Robert, had died. Young Robert was only seventeen and was an able talented lad who had shown great promise. Oliver was shattered.

'It went as a dagger through my heart,' he said.

• • • • •

For eleven years, King Charles had ruled without his Parliament. However, a disastrous attempt to force a new prayer book on the stubborn Scots had resulted in a costly war. Once again, Charles needed money. So, once again, he had to summon Parliament.

Since he was now living in Ely, Oliver could no longer represent Huntingdon. However, he was eligible to be elected for Cambridge, but first he had to become a free-man of the city. His many friends persuaded the Mayor of Cambridge that Oliver would make a very suitable freeman. Oliver was sworn in looking very smart in a new red coat, trimmed with gold lace. To celebrate, he provided wine and sweetmeats and whilst these were being enjoyed, his friends and supporters spread the word that he would make an excellent candidate in the forthcoming election. Oliver was duly elected! So, Oliver once more made the journey to London.

In his efforts to raise money without Parliament's help, Charles had managed to upset a lot of people. When Parliament met in April, 1640, it was not happy and it was certainly not ready to give the king the money he needed until he had agreed to their demands.

It was a short stay in London. As usual the king and

Parliament could not agree and once again the king dissolved Parliament. The session had only lasted three weeks and so it became known as the Short Parliament.

However, Charles still had a problem with the Scots and he needed money to persuade their army to return to Scotland. He had no choice except to recall Parliament. There was another election and in October, Oliver once again made the journey south to represent Cambridge in what was to become known as the Long Parliament.

By now, Oliver was one of the better known MPs. Many of his friends and relations, such as his cousin, John Hampden, were also MPs. Most of those elected were very unhappy at the way King Charles was ruling the country. Parliament was now ready to take on the King and make him change some of his policies.

Oliver was very busy. He was appointed to many committees, particularly those which discussed religious matters. He had gained confidence and now people took notice of him when he spoke in the House.

He was not a gifted speaker. He was far too blunt and straightforward for that. However, there was no doubt that he was sincere and ready to defend those who he felt were being treated unfairly. As a Puritan, he was against the changes Charles had made to the Church of England and he spoke out very strongly against the Church's policies and the king's interference in religious matters.

Other MPs began to notice the well-built figure dressed in a plain cloth suit. He was not a smart dresser. There was occasionally a speck of blood on his neck band as he often shaved in a hurry. He would wear a hat without a hat band and when he spoke his face would look swollen and reddish. His voice was rather sharp and untuneful.

'Who is that man who has just spoken?' Lord Digby asked John Hampden after one debate.

'That untidy fellow which you see before us, who hath no ornament in his speech.' replied Hampden. 'I say that sloven if we should come to have a breach with the King (which God forbid) in such case will be one of the greatest men in England.' Little did he know how true his words would turn out to be.

Oliver was definitely a man to be reckoned with.

CHAPTER SIX

TENSION MOUNTS

During the next fifteen months, tension increased between the king and Parliament and England moved closer and closer to Civil War.

Parliament accused the king's friend and closest adviser, the Earl of Strafford of high treason and Charles had no choice but to have him executed.

Parliament then forced the king to agree to a series of reforms which completely changed the way the king could rule the country.

In 1641 there was a rebellion in Ireland and news reached England that many English and Scottish Protestants had been massacred by the Irish Catholics. Many of these reports were exaggerated, but many people were again afraid of a Catholic plot and shouts of 'No Popery!' and 'Down with the Queen!' could be heard in the streets.

Parliament then passed the Grand Remonstrance which was a document listing all the wrongs that the king had inflicted on the country. They even tried to take control of the army away from the him.

This was the last straw. Many people now felt that Parliament was going too far and they were afraid that the Puritans were becoming too powerful. The country started to feel sorry for the king. Charles became confident and then he made a big mistake . . .

It was a cold day in January 1642. Parliament was in session. Oliver was amongst those in the House of Commons. Suddenly there was a loud knock at the door.

'His Majesty demands entry,' announced an officer. The MPs were shocked. No monarch in English history had ever set foot in the House of Commons.

King Charles strode into the chamber, a slight figure. He had come to arrest five leading MPs. There was a stunned silence but the MPs did not forget their manners. They took off their high crowned, broad brimmed hats.

'By your leave, Mr Speaker.' said the king. 'I must borrow your chair a little.' He sat down and looked around the chamber. He quickly realised that the five men he sought were no longer there. They had been warned and had already left by a back door, escaping into a boat which took them to a safe place. They had left the king to make a fool of himself.

Charles demanded an explanation.

'I have eyes to see and ears to hear as the House may direct,' replied the Speaker respectfully.

'Tis no matter,' said Charles. 'I think my eyes are as good as another's. I see the birds have flown.'

Oliver watched as the embarrassed king turned and walked out of the Chamber.

It was the end. King and Parliament no longer trusted each other. Both sides started to gather support and to prepare their troops for war.

Oliver returned to East Anglia. He had a very important job to do – to raise a troop of cavalry and to make sure that Cambridge did not fall into Royalist hands.

CHAPTER SEVEN

PREPARING FOR WAR

In many ways a Civil War is the worst kind of war. It sets father against son, friend against friend and turns neighbours into enemies.

People had to decide which side they supported. Were they for King or for Parliament? Some found it a very difficult decision to make.

'The great God who is the searcher of my heart knows with what reluctance I go upon this service and with what perfect hatred I look upon this war without an enemy.' Thus spoke Sir William Waller who supported Parliament as his great friend Sir Ralph Hopton became King Charles' commander in the West of England.

Oliver had no such doubts. He had already decided that war was the only way to sort out the quarrels that were tearing the country apart. It was his duty to support the Parliamentary cause even if this meant waging war on his king.

East Anglia was strongly for Parliament. It would contribute most of the Parliament's troops and after London, most of the money to fight the war. If it had not been for the strong support of East Anglia, Parliament would have found it very difficult to win.

However, since most of the University supported the king, Oliver had to make sure that the city of Cambridge was held for Parliament. The County of Cambridgeshire and the Isle of Ely were placed in the care of Oliver and Sir Dudley Norton.

Oliver wasted no time. He put the town in a state of defence. Earthworks were thrown up around the castle. All bridges except the Great Bridge were destroyed. Houses around the castle were pulled down and arms and armour inside the castle were seized. Timber and stone set aside by Clare Hall for new buildings were used to build defences.

Later on, one of the courts of St. John's College became a prison and King's College Chapel was a drill hall. Although it was not Oliver's intention, he managed to prevent the magnificent stained glass windows from being destroyed, but the troops carved graffiti onto the stone walls.

Arms were sent into the town for both sides, but when fifteen chests of arms arrived from London for the Royalists, Oliver made sure that these were seized for Parliament.

By now, he had raised a troop of sixty horsemen. He was busy arming and training them. Some of the equipment was paid for out of his own pocket. His son, Oliver, had also volunteered for the cavalry. Oliver gave him permission to join, but made him join another troop as he felt that it would be better if he served under another commander.

The king desperately needed money to buy weapons. He wrote to the Cambridge Colleges, suggesting that their silver plate should be sent to him for safekeeping. Not all the Colleges agreed with this suggestion, but some gathered together a quantity of valuables and prepared to send them to the king.

Someone leaked the plan to Oliver and he was determined that the plate should not reach its destination. Helped by his brother-in-law, Valentine Walton, he blocked the road north, hiding his soldiers in the cornfields on either side of the road. Needless to say, the plate never reached the king!

• • • • •

It was a bitterly cold day in October, 1642. The two armies were to meet for the first time at Edgehill in the Midlands. Oliver was there with his small troop of cavalry. The armies were lined up. The Royalists were in position near the bottom of the hill, facing the Parliamentary army under the command of the Earl of Essex.

It was a brave sight. Thousands of men in different coloured coats and an assorted array of armour waiting for the battle to begin.

The pikemen were placed in the centre ready to take the brunt of the fighting. They held their sixteen foot pikes tightly and nervously, waiting for the cavalry charge.

Near them were the musketeers. Their weapons were clumsy and so heavy that they needed a stand to support them when they fired. They took so long to reload that the men knew that they would have to use their muskets like clubs when the enemy got close and hand to hand fighting broke out. The measures of gunpowder dangled from the bandoliers across their chests and the tapers glowed gently in their hands.

The cavalry were ready on either side of the foot soldiers,

dressed in light armour, swords ready, pistols cocked, horses alert, waiting for the signal to charge.

It came. Prince Rupert, the king's nephew, led his cavalry in a devastating charge at, then straight through, the Parliamentary foot soldiers, slashing at them with swords, firing pistols and scattering men before them. It was terrifying. The foot soldiers hesitated, broke ranks and then fled.

Once into the charge, Rupert could not stop his men and gather them together for another charge. They galloped off the field of battle towards the village of Kineton four miles away. Whilst they were away, the Parliamentarians and their cavalry attacked the Royalist foot soldiers.

By the time Rupert and his men returned, the battle was nearly over. It was dark and both sides were exhausted. Neither side had won, it was a draw.

About fifteen hundred men died that day. Amongst them was the king's standard bearer, Sir Edmund Verney. He held onto his standard to the bitter end and they had to chop his hand off to get possession of it. Many more would have died of cold for it was a freezing night, but the wounded pulled the bodies of the dead on top of them to give them some warmth and so they survived until morning.

Although Oliver took part in the fighting, he was not involved in the main part of the battle. He had time to look and learn. He saw that if Rupert had been able to control his men and charge the enemy again, the king could have won the battle. He also saw that Parliament would never win the war unless it had a well-trained cavalry.

'Your troopers are, most of them, old decayed serving men,' he wrote to his cousin Hampden. 'Their troopers are gentlemen's sons, younger sons and persons of quality. You must get men of spirit that is likely to go as far as gentlemen will, or else I am sure you will be beaten still.'

Oliver returned to East Anglia. He began to recruit his 'men of spirit' from the villages and towns near his home.

And from these 'men of spirit' were fashioned Oliver Cromwell's famous 'Ironsides'.

CHAPTER EIGHT

OLIVER'S IRONSIDES

There was no shortage of recruits. Farmers, carpenters, labourers and many others came to join Oliver's troops. He wanted 'honest, godly men' who 'had the fear of God before them'. They had to believe in what they were fighting for and most of them were Puritan like their leader. He chose his officers carefully for 'if you choose honest godly men, honest men will follow them'. Many of the officers were friends or relations, men he could trust.

Not everyone agreed with Oliver's ideas. Some complained later on that he was appointing officers who were not gentlemen. Oliver had no patience with such complaints. 'I had rather have a plain russet-coated captain that knows what he fights for and loves what he knows, than that which you call a gentleman and is nothing else,' he retorted sharply. He was never one to suffer fools gladly!

Discipline was strict and training was hard. Swearing was punished by a twelve pence fine, drunks would be put in the stocks and plundering was not allowed. Two soldiers who tried to desert were whipped in Huntingdon market place.

Oliver read books on warfare and training and then put

his own ideas into practice. His men had to be totally obedient on the field of battle. Once they had charged, they had to be able to stop, re-form and charge again. Orders had to be obeyed without question.

You cannot have a cavalry without horses and Oliver cared deeply for his horses. Every day his troopers had to look after their horses, clean their arms and armour and be ready. Not everyone was accepted and he would turn away those who proved unsuitable. As a test, he and a few others charged at a group of new recruits, pretending it was an ambush. Those who ran away were instantly dismissed. His Ironsides had to be strong and resolute. They had to be the best.

Within a year, he had raised and trained ten troops of cavalry – a thousand men – and this was soon increased to fourteen troops of cavalry. They looked very tough in their leather buff coats which kept out the rain. Their leather boots which reached to the thigh were made waterproof by rubbing with a tallow beeswax mixture and to give them added protection they wore a metal back and breast plate, and on their head a helmet, known as a 'pot' (for obvious reasons). They were each armed with a sword and two pistols and across their chests was an orange sash. The Royalist cavalry wore red sashes.

Although Oliver was very strict, he was also very popular with his men. He would laugh and joke with them and ask after their families. After training, he would share a drink with them. They would pray together and listen to sermons on Sundays. Eventually each soldier carried a pocket Bible next to his heart. This contained extracts from the Bible, usually about battles and victory.

After Edgehill, the king failed to capture London which

he had to do if he was to win the war. He therefore decided on a pincer movement to capture the capital. His army in the north under the Earl of Newcastle would move down towards London. At the same time Sir Ralph Hopton and his brave band of Cornishmen should move up from the west with the result that London would be under attack from two directions.

To prevent this, it was essential that Parliament held onto East Anglia. Oliver wasted no time in giving his newly trained troops plenty of chances to practise what he had taught them.

1643 was a busy year. In January Oliver and a few troopers were passing through St Albans. The High Sheriff of Hertfordshire was in the market place, drumming up support for the king. He was protected by Royalist troops. 'This is not to be tolerated,' cried Oliver. After a fierce struggle, the Sheriff was taken prisoner and sent to the Tower.

In March, Oliver and his troops seemed to be everywhere. In the space of ten days, he rode from Cambridge to Norwich, on to Yarmouth and Lowestoft, back to Norwich, to King's Lynn and finally back to Cambridge.

As he went, he put down Royalist resistance, seized arms and valuables for Parliament and collected contributions and recruits.

A month later, he was involved in the siege of Croyland, near Peterborough. Then in May, he and his troops were near Grantham. Suddenly, they came across a huge Royalist force with nearly twice the number of men. Oliver had to make a quick decision. It would be wiser to withdraw, but he trusted his men and it was a good opportunity to see if they had learned their lessons well.

The Ironsides advanced at a fast trot. The enemy stood firm. The Ironsides charged and the enemy fled. Only two of Oliver's men were killed and a hundred of the king's.

It was the Ironsides' first victorious charge.

• • • • •

Further victories followed.

Stamford was captured and Peterborough was defended. In July, Oliver led a siege on Burghley House in Stamford and took it with no loss of life. Following this, he moved onto Gainsborough where there was a fierce 'hand to hand' or rather 'horse to horse' battle which Oliver won. However, after the battle, when both men and horses were exhausted, the news came that the Earl of Newcastle's army had arrived, ready to do battle. Oliver knew that Gainsborough could not be held against such a great force and so he gave the order to retreat.

Oliver knew he had to retreat in an orderly manner or many of his men would be killed. This was not an easy task as the enemy was already attacking them. Tired and exhausted he formed his men into a group and then ordered them to fire and retreat, fire and retreat. The Ironsides stood firm. The retreat was successfully completed.

The two most difficult problems that a cavalry commander has to face are to attack an enemy which is greater in number and already drawn up for battle and to retreat when facing an army which is fresh and has more men.

At Gainsborough, Oliver did both.

His Ironsides had proved themselves. Oliver was rewarded by being made Governor of the Isle of Ely and one of the four colonels under the Earl of Manchester who was commander of the Eastern Association.

Commanding troops was not all battles. When not fighting, Oliver was busy writing letters, both for extra men and for money to pay his troops. He wrote countless letters to the authorities urging them to send the cash so that he could buy clothes and equipment for his men. He paid for shoes, stockings and shirts for some troops out of his own pocket.

In October, at Winceby in Lincolnshire he met the man who was later to be his chief. This was Sir Thomas Fairfax, known as 'Black Tom'. They got on well and fought together for the first time in the battle that followed.

Oliver led the first charge against the Royalists, spurring his horse to a full gallop. Suddenly his horse collapsed underneath him, killed by a pistol ball. Stunned, Oliver got to his feet, only to be knocked down again. Once more he got up and seized another horse. He remounted and fought on. The Royalists fled. A few weeks later Lincolnshire was in Parliament's hands.

The winter of 1643 was spent quietly with his family in Ely. He was delighted when his eldest daughter, Bridget, became engaged to Henry Ireton, one of his officers.

He had plenty to do. There were funds to raise and recruits to gather. He also had to make sure that the Cathedral in Ely was free of the elaborate ornaments, ceremonies and even choirs which the Puritans so disliked.

He was none too pleased to discover that Reverend Henry Hitch was conducting choir services in the Cathedral. Oliver wrote a short, polite note asking him to

stop. He even signed it 'your loving friend'. Mr Hitch made the mistake of ignoring the letter.

As Mr Hitch was conducting one of his choir services, Oliver strode into the Cathedral. 'I am a man under authority and I am commanded to dismiss this assembly,' Oliver announced. Mr Hitch hesitated and then continued. 'Leave off your fooling and come down sir.'

No-one disobeyed that harsh commanding voice. Mr Hitch came down.

There was sadness too. Oliver's son, also called Oliver, died when smallpox swept through his barracks. Oliver had now lost his second son.

CHAPTER NINE

THE WAR IS WON

Apart from East Anglia, 1643 had not been a good year for Parliament as the Royalists had been successful elsewhere. Parliament was scared of losing the war and they therefore signed an agreement with the Scots. In return for military help, Parliament agreed that the English Church should become Presbyterian like the Scots. Not all MPs agreed. Oliver and those like him were 'Independents' and they believed in freedom of worship. They did not want to see Presbyterianism in England. To avoid a quarrel, Oliver signed the agreement or Covenant (as it was called). Luckily the wording was rather vague and it was agreed that the matter should be discussed again after the war.

Thus it was that on 2nd July, 1644, a Scottish army joined the Parliamentary army to face the Royalists at Marston Moor near York.

Prince Rupert, the King's brilliant cavalry commander was keen to see the Ironsides in action. 'Is Cromwell here?' he asked eagerly before the battle.

Parliament had more men, but the Royalists had a better position. The moor looked like a sea of different coloured waves. There were the bright banners and the different coloured coats of each regiment for there was no common uniform. In the heat of battle it was difficult to tell friend from foe so battle signs were adopted. On this occasion the Parliamentary soldiers wore a piece of white paper or rag in their helmets.

Both sides faced each other all day. From the Parliamentary side the singing of psalms could be heard. Then Rupert decided that it was too late to fight that day and he stood his men down. Since he was hungry he went to have his supper and his fellow commander, the Marquis of Newcastle, relaxed in his carriage, smoking his pipe.

There was a loud thunderclap. The sky turned black and heavy rain began to fall. The Ironsides began to move – short reins and short stirrups, riding close together at a fast trot. Horrified, the Royalists watched as the top of the hill seemed to move towards them.

Rupert dashed onto the field, leaving his supper unfinished, gathering together as many of his men as possible as he went. They charged at Oliver and his Ironsides. It was a terrible battle. Both sides hacked at each other with their swords and the air was full of the cries of those fighting and the screams of the dying. 'God is with us,' yelled the Roundheads. 'God and King,' shouted the Royalists. Many of the dead were trampled in the mud underfoot.

In the middle of the battle, Oliver was wounded in the neck. Luckily it was only a flesh wound, but he had to leave the field for a short time to have it dressed. Whilst he was away, the Ironsides were nearly scattered by Rupert's cavalry. Sir Thomas Fairfax was separated from his men and found himself completely surrounded by the enemy. He calmly removed the white rag from his helmet and shook out his long black hair. Looking like a cavalier, he made his way through the enemy lines to the safety of his own side. By this time the Parliamentary side was in great trouble. It looked as if they were going to lose the battle. Oliver returned and quickly realised the danger. He rallied his Ironsides. They charged, they reformed, they charged again.

A final charge from the rear was too much for the Royal-

ists, but Newcastle's loyal Whitecoats refused to surrender. They stood in the centre of the field, fighting to the last man, their white coats stained red with their blood.

Rupert escaped by hiding in a bean field, but his dog, Boy, was not so lucky. He had followed Rupert onto the field of battle and had been killed.

'We never charged, but we routed the enemy ... God made them as stubble to our swords,' said Oliver afterwards.

It was after this battle that Prince Rupert gave the name 'Ironsides' to Oliver and his men.

It was an overwhelming victory. The king had lost the North, but it would take one more battle for him to lose the war.

• • • • •

Unfortunately, Parliament failed to build upon Oliver's success at Marston Moor. Oliver felt that the fault lay mainly with his commanding officer, the Earl of Manchester. He seemed unwilling to inflict a total defeat on the king. 'If we beat the king ninety nine times, he would be king still, but if he beats us once we should be hanged,' Manchester cried.

'My Lord, if this be so, why did we take up arms at first?' Oliver replied.

Oliver was never one to mince his words and he expressed his views strongly. Manchester accused him of being a troublemaker. A bitter quarrel looked likely and this would split Parliament.

Oliver's only aim was to win the war for Parliament, so he took a more tactful path.

It had been suggested that the Parliamentary army should be reorganised. Oliver pressed for this and went further by proposing that no MP should hold any office or command in the army. This meant that Manchester, the Earl of Essex and Oliver could no longer be in the army.

This was a clever move. The New Model Army came into being. Instead of being organised and paid locally, it was controlled centrally by Parliament. Its General was Sir Thomas Fairfax. The post of second in command and head of the cavalry was not filled. Everyone knew why. Oliver was the best cavalry commander they had and they could not win without him. Parliament had to make an exception with the result that Manchester and Essex resigned their commands and Oliver was left as the only MP to hold office in the army.

So, in May 1645, Oliver was to be found spurring his horse on. His six hundred men followed him. The rest had been left behind in Cambridge. They were on their way to join Black Tom Fairfax at Kislingbury, near the village of Naseby, in Northamptonshire. Oliver had been in Cambridge when he heard that the two armies were about to meet. Would he be in time?

Oliver and his men reached Fairfax's camp. A great shout of joy went up 'Ironsides is come,' they yelled.

The battle lines were formed. Black Tom looked at his troops in their new red coats. Many of them were new recruits, nervous before their first battle. He would need the strength and experience of Oliver and his Ironsides if he was to win.

The battle was fierce. The king's army fought bravely, but the men of the New Model Army were too many and

Oliver's Ironsides were too strong. They charged, reformed, charged, reformed. They were like an iron wall which could not be dented. It was an overwhelming victory for Parliament. The king lost the war on the battlefield at Naseby.

● ● ● ● ●

It was March 1646 when the last handful of the king's army surrendered at Stow on the Wold.

'You have done your work, boys and may go and play, unless you will fall out among yourselves.' said a Royalist officer to his captor.

CHAPTER TEN

THE QUARRELS START

And fall out they did. Once the war was won, the members of Parliament started to quarrel amongst themselves. They quarrelled about religion and the king.

The king escaped to Scotland, but was sent back to England in return for £400,000. Charles continued his old tricks, playing one side off against the other and encouraging his captors to fall out amongst themselves.

Oliver was well rewarded for all his successes. He received money and land and was now a rich man. His eldest daughters were married and Oliver wanted to return to his Parliamentary duties. He moved to Drury Lane in London with his wife, mother and four younger children. His Ely house was let to one of his servants.

Trouble was brewing in the New Model Army. The soldiers had not been paid and they were restless. A clash between Parliament and the army was likely because although they were all Protestants, most of the army were 'Independents' and most of Parliament was Presbyterian. Oliver was caught in the middle.

He loved his soldiers who had served him so loyally and so well. He felt that Parliament was treating them very badly. On the other hand he was a little worried that some of the soldiers were becoming rather too independent. He had the difficult task of trying to bring both sides together. As always, when facing a difficult problem, he prayed to God for help and guidance.

Parliament planned to send part of the army to Ireland to fight the Irish Catholics, and to dismiss the rest. They snubbed Oliver by not choosing him as one of the commanding officers. The soldiers who were gathered at Saffron Walden were furious.

'Why not our old generals? Fairfax and Cromwell and we all go,' they cried. Oliver tried to keep the soldiers calm.

The king watched and waited. It was not long before both Oliver and Parliament realised that he was the most important piece in a tricky game of chess.

The king was being held at Holdenby House. On a fine June day in 1646, he was in the garden enjoying the sunshine. Suddenly, hoofbeats were heard and a soldier called Cornet Joyce at the head of five hundred troopers arrived with orders to make sure that the king was safe and secure. It is very likely that he was acting on Oliver's instructions.

Having made sure that the king was safe in his hands, Cornet Joyce was not sure what to do next. He decided that he ought to move him closer to the army who were gathered near Newmarket. The king was happy to go with the soldiers and asked them to take him to his hunting lodge at Newmarket.

The Presbyterian MPs were furious and they decided to arrest Oliver. Oliver acted quickly. He rode swiftly to the army at Newmarket and threw his lot in with them.

Oliver now had an important decision to make. He was forty eight years old and tired after fighting for many years. It would be easy to retire to Ely with his family and spend his last years in peace and comfort. But his duty and conscience would not allow him to take the easy path. He could not leave the country in chaos after so many people had died. He must work for a responsible government in England, perhaps with the king at its head.

The army marched to London and the king was taken to Hampton Court. With the 'independent' soldiers at the door of the House of Commons, the Presbyterian MPs thought it wiser to leave! Oliver became a juggler, dealing with all sides at once – the king, the agitators in his army and Parliament.

He continued his discussions with the king hoping to agree on a form of government with Charles at its head.

The army continued to be a problem. The soldiers realised that they were now a powerful force. Many of the soldiers were 'Levellers' and they wanted everyone to be equal before the law and to have the right to vote. Nowadays, this sounds very reasonable, but three hundred years ago it was unheard of. Those, like Oliver, who already owned property were not keen to see those who had no property at all have the same privileges.

Oliver realised that some of the soldiers were becoming stubborn and dangerous. Some of the agitators began to preach open revolt.

After several meetings and many hours of argument, Oliver lost patience with his rebellious men. At a further meeting in Ware in November 1647, the Leveller soldiers arrived with the motto 'England's freedom! Soldiers' right!' stuck in their hats and two regiments who had not been invited, turned up. Oliver was furious at their disobedience.

'Remove your tokens,' he ordered. The men refused. Oliver did not hesitate. He drew his sword and rode amongst them, knocking the tokens to the ground. The four ringleaders were arrested and after casting lots, one was shot as an example to the rest.

At the same time, news arrived that Charles had escaped from Hampton Court to the Isle of Wight and was now negotiating with the Scots. The second Civil War was about to start.

•••••

Early in 1648, the Royalists rose in Wales, Kent and Essex. The navy declared for the king and the Scots invaded England in support of Charles.

The fighting did not last long. By November it was nearly over. Oliver and his Ironsides put down the rising in Wales. They then had to march north without shoes or stockings until further provisions reached them at Leicester. They defeated the Scots at Preston and War-rington. By October, Oliver was in Edinburgh and the Scots were beaten.

However, the Royalists still held Pontefract so Oliver marched south again to lay siege to the town. Whilst he was there the news leaked out that Parliament had started negotiating again with the king.

This time the army had had enough. Charles could no longer be trusted. They had sworn that when the fighting was over they would call 'Charles Stuart, that man of blood to an account for that blood he had shed and mischief he had done.'

They seized the king in the Isle of Wight. They marched on London. A certain Colonel Pride stood at the entrance to the House of Commons, a list in his hands, and stopped all the MPs who were in favour of a treaty with the king from entering Parliament.

By the time Oliver reached London, the army was in control and Charles was about to be put on trial for his life.

The trial was held in January 1649. It was a public trial and fully reported in all the newspapers of the day.

Charles was accused of being 'a tyrant traitor and murderer and a public and implacable enemy to the Commonwealth of England.'

Oliver and the other sixty seven members in the court took their places. A roll call was held and there was no answer when Sir Thomas Fairfax's name was called.

'He has more wit than to be here,' shouted a masked lady from the gallery. It was Lady Fairfax, his wife. Although Tom Fairfax had supported the decision to try the king and had attended earlier meetings, he was not prepared to be one of the judges. Lady Fairfax was a Presbyterian and was certainly against the trial.

Oliver looked at Charles. He was dressed entirely in black, his hair was grey and he looked old and tired. He held a silver topped cane in his hand. The head of the cane rolled onto the floor. When no-one moved, the king bent down and picked it up.

The charges were read and Charles was asked to answer them. All his life the king had stammered but now, facing a court which would condemn him to death, he spoke clearly and without any hesitation.

'I would know by what power I am called hither,' he said coldly. There was no doubt that the Court intended to find him guilty, but they had not expected Charles to be so brave and dignified. 'God save the king. God bless you sir,' called some of the crowd and even some of the soldiers.

When the President reminded the Court that the king had been charged with treason in the name of the people of England, Lady Fairfax shouted, 'Not half, not a quarter of the people of England. Oliver Cromwell is a traitor.'

The sentence of death was passed. The king asked to be heard. The President refused. John Downes, one of the members of the court was sitting behind Oliver.

'Have we hearts of stone? Are we men? Let him speak,' he called. Oliver turned round.

'What ails thee man. Art thou mad? Canst thou not sit still and be quiet,' he hissed.

Downes got to his feet. 'Sir, no I cannot be quiet, I am not satisfied.' But it made no difference.

Oliver's was one of the fifty nine signatures on the death warrant. On January 30th 1649, Charles I was beheaded. He had put on two vests because it was a cold day and he did not want the crowd to think that he was shivering because he was afraid. He died with dignity.

CHAPTER ELEVEN

LONG LIVE THE KING

England was now a Commonwealth and Free State. A special seal was made to show this. On one side was the House of Commons full of MPs and on the other was a map showing England, Wales and Ireland, but no Scotland as it was not part of the Commonwealth. The seal cost £200 to produce.

In the years that followed, Oliver was not to find peace. In fact he had a lot more fighting to do.

The Levellers were once again stirring up trouble in the army. They were furious that the execution of the king had not altered the way the country was governed and not given more power to ordinary people. Their leaders were arrested and brought before the Council of State. Oliver was quite clear at what had to be done.

'I tell you sir you have no other way to deal with these men but to break them or they will break you,' he shouted, thumping on the table. The leaders were sent to the Tower. Oliver felt some sadness. One of them, John Lilburne, had been a friend and a fellow soldier. Were all his friends to become enemies?

Parts of the army mutinied. The two commanders, Oliver and Tom Fairfax, moved quickly. They marched fifty miles in one day and caught the mutineers napping.

Three were executed and the other risings were put down.

There was again trouble in Ireland. Royalists had joined together with some of the Irish Catholics and were now a great threat to England. Oliver was seen as the only person who could restore order. He was made Commander in Chief and in July 1649 he set sail. It was a rough crossing and Oliver was very seasick.

In those days Ireland was a wild place. Roads were poor, there were pirates around the coast and wolves inland. Public wolf hunts were held and £6 was paid for each wolf.

Oliver believed that he was going into battle against an army of vicious and cruel Catholics. He reached the town of Drogheda and asked that it should surrender peacefully.

'If this be refused, you will have no cause to blame me,' he said warningly. Sir Arthur Aston, the Royalist commander refused and thus took a big risk. He knew what the penalty could be. If Drogheda was taken by force, then it could expect no mercy as a lesson to other towns who might be tempted to hold out. These were the rules of war at that time.

No mercy was shown in Drogheda. Usually Oliver was a merciful man, but when he took Drogheda he was very angry. The defenders were slaughtered. Two thousand soldiers were killed, not a priest remained alive. Many civilians got in the way and were killed as well. About three thousand were dead at the end of the day. Poor Sir Arthur Aston was beaten to death with his wooden leg.

Several other Irish towns were so horrified that they surrendered without a fight, but Wexford made the mistake of trying to hold out. Whilst negotiations appeared to be going on, Oliver's troops broke through the city walls and ran amok. About two thousand people were killed, many of them drowned whilst trying to escape.

A messenger arrived from England; Oliver was now needed at home. He left his son-in-law, Ireton, to finish off in Ireland and set sail. As he made his way to London he was greeted by cheering crowds. He was a hero in England, but in Ireland he had left behind an atmosphere of hate which was to last for hundreds of years.

The news at home was not good. The Scots had been horrified by the execution of Charles I for he was their king as well. They had lost no time in proclaiming his son, also called Charles, their rightful king. A Scottish army was now ready to invade England and put Charles II on the throne.

The Scots were no more successful than the Irish. Oliver defeated the Scottish army at Dunbar. It was a brilliant victory. The Scots had twice as many men and had trapped Oliver and his army.

'We have much hope in the Lord,' prayed Oliver. Indeed God seemed to answer his prayer. The Scottish army moved to a new position, giving Oliver the chance to attack.

'The Lord of Hosts' was his battle cry as his army swept down at dawn. 'Now let God arise and his enemies shall be scattered,' he shouted in the middle of the battle.

And scattered they were. Three thousand died, ten thousand were taken prisoner and Oliver lost only twenty men. It seemed to be a miracle. Medals were struck to celebrate the victory. The high ranking officers received a gold one, the junior officers a silver one and the soldiers got two copper ones. But the fight had weakened Oliver and for several months he was very ill with fever. At one point, it was feared that he might die. However, he made a slow recovery and delayed leaving Scotland until he was fit again.

There was one more battle. Charles II had marched south, gathering an army as he went. Oliver followed him and the two armies met at Worcester in September 1651. Oliver knew that this was one battle he must not lose. Throughout the fighting he could be seen riding through the cannon fire, urging his men on.

The Royalists were totally defeated. Oliver returned to London, once more the great hero. Charles II escaped to France despite a price of £1000 on his head.

It was to be nine years before Charles returned to England again to claim his throne.

CHAPTER TWELVE

MY LORD PROTECTOR

It was about 11.15 in the morning and the House of Commons was crowded. The door opened and Oliver rushed in. He was obviously in a great hurry as he was dressed very informally in a black coat and grey stockings. He sat in his place for a few minutes listening to what was being discussed.

Suddenly he stood up and started to speak. He was in a rage.

'I will put an end to your prating. You are no Parliament. I say you are no Parliament. I will put an end to your sitting,' he stormed. With that, the door opened again and about twenty musketeers came in. Oliver pointed to the Speaker.

'Fetch him down,' he ordered. The Speaker was removed. Oliver then picked up the mace. 'What shall we do with this bauble? Here take it away.' He looked at the rest of the horrified MPs. 'It is you that have forced me to do this', he said bitterly. His soldiers then made the rest of the MPs leave the chamber.

Oliver had just dissolved what was known as the 'Rump' Parliament. This had been very unpopular for some time since it had talked and argued but had done very little. Both the army and Oliver had lost patience with it. The

Rump had promised to hold fresh elections, but Oliver had discovered that it had no intention of keeping that promise.

The next Parliament was not a great success either, since many of its members were extremely religious. They claimed that they had received an extraordinary call from Christ and they spent most of their time either making or listening to long rambling speeches. It was known as the 'Barebones' Parliament after one of its members who was called 'Praise be to God Barebones'!

By December 1653, the moderate members of the Barebones Parliament had lost patience. They resigned their authority into Oliver's hands and four days later he became Lord Protector. He took his oath of office dressed in black velvet with a gold band around his hat. He was now fifty four years old. His face was ruddy and lined and his hair was grey. He was an impressive, but lonely figure.

Oliver now ruled England with an elected Parliament which would meet for five months once every three years. In his speech to his first Parliament Oliver said he hoped that it would be a time of healing. For years, it had been 'Overturn, overturn and overturn.' He had not chosen to be Lord Protector, but now that he was, he intended to do his duty to the best of his ability.

Oliver and his family moved into the Palace of Whitehall. They would spend the weekdays there and travel out to Hampton Court at weekends. He wanted to spend more time with his family. Very sadly, there had been two more deaths. The first was his son-in-law and friend, Henry Ireton who died of the plague. The second was his mother who died at the grand age of eighty nine. His two youngest daughters, Mary and Frances, were now engaged and his sons, Richard and Henry, were married. Oliver still worried about Richard. He was not a strong character and Oliver thought he was easily led. He tended to mix with unsuitable people and get himself into debt.

He and Elizabeth were still very happy together. Elizabeth would have preferred a simpler life, back in Ely, but Oliver was her husband so she made the best of things. She continued to sew and kept a close eye on the household finances. She showed an interest in art and started collecting pictures. Oliver still enjoyed hunting and hawking. He liked to entertain old friends casually over a tankard of beer and a simple meal and he still found time to go for picnics.

It was at one picnic that he very nearly lost his life. After he had eaten he tried out a new present – a team of four splendid horses. The horses took fright and threw both Oliver and the groom. Oliver was dragged some way by his foot and in the confusion a pistol went off. Luckily, he suffered no worse than an injured leg.

● ● ● ● ●

The job of Lord Protector was neither an easy nor peaceful one. There were many things that Oliver enjoyed and he was proud that he managed to achieve several successes. He did a lot for education – many free schools were started, university education was encouraged and he welcomed scientific discoveries. He allowed everyone to worship without interference as long as they did not plot against the government. As a result of his foreign policies, England's navy grew strong and was respected abroad.

He was given presents by people who wanted to make a good impression. It was well known that he loved riding and hawking and he was given both hawks and horses. He was very pleased with a small cabinet given to him by the Grand Duke of Tuscany. It was a beautiful piece of craftsmanship. It was made of ebony and walnut and inlaid with hard stone. The sides were decorated with fruit and birds and the top had a picture of a cart by a building. Its three drawers contained small glass pots with decorated covers.

Unfortunately, his Parliament proved very difficult. It could not agree and spent most of its time quarrelling. Oliver believed that it was very important for the Protector to appear to be strong and powerful, but many people thought that he and his family were getting too big for their boots and were behaving like the Royal family. The Royalists stirred up ill feeling by mocking Elizabeth Cromwell for not being grand enough, and then they poked fun at Oliver for having too many servants, grand coaches and elaborate ceremonies. Poor Oliver could not win either way!

There were several plots against his life. As a result of these plots, Oliver had to become very strict. In 1655 he divided the country into twelve districts and put a Major-General in charge of each one. Their job was to make sure that there was law and order in the country. Many of these men tried to enforce a strict Puritan way of life and they became very unpopular.

Ordinary people had had enough of fighting and arguing and they wanted to live in peace and enjoy themselves. Under the Major-Generals this was very difficult. Horse racing, bear baiting, cock fighting, and gambling were forbidden. Christmas and May day could not be celebrated in an enjoyable way. There were cases of May poles being chopped down and Christmas dinners being taken away by soldiers. Certain ale houses and taverns were closed down. On Sundays, people were expected to go to church and spend the rest of the day quietly at home. They were certainly not allowed to do any sport or anything which might be considered fun. Anyone breaking these laws could be fined, whipped, put in the stocks or in prison.

No wonder many people thought Oliver was spoiling their fun, particularly since it was known that he enjoyed music, jokes, singing and the odd tankard of beer.

The Major Generals only lasted about eighteen months. Fairly soon afterwards, Oliver was asked to be king.

He thought about it for some time. 'I am sorry to have caused so much time and trouble,' he said 'but I cannot accept the title of king.' He was appointed Lord Protector for a second time and was allowed to choose someone to succeed him after his death.

By now Oliver was not well. The past years had been hard and the problems of ruling the country were sapping his strength. In August 1658 his favourite daughter Bettie died. Oliver was heartbroken and he never really got over her death.

George Fox, the Quaker leader met him in Hyde Park and was horrified. 'I saw and felt a waft of death go forth against him,' he wrote in his journal.

On 3rd September, 1658, the anniversary of two of his greatest victories, Worcester and Dunbar, he slipped into a coma and died. He was buried in Westminster Abbey.

Nearly two years later in the spring of 1660, Charles II landed in England, having been invited back to take his throne.

A little later, some Royalists dug up Oliver's body, publicly hanged it and put his skull on a pole for all to see.

• • • • •

It was not a fitting end for the man from East Anglia.

PLACES TO VISIT

HUNTINGDON
Hinchingbrooke House, the site of Cromwell's house (now the Cromwell Clinic) and the George Inn. Cromwell's school is now the Cromwell Museum. Many of the items mentioned in this book, such as the seal of the Commonwealth and the cabinet given by the Grand Duke of Tuscany, can be seen here.

ST IVES

ELY
The Cathedral and Cromwell's house which is now the Tourist Information Office.

THE TOWER OF LONDON
Visit the Armoury to see the arms used in the Civil War.

BURGHLEY HOUSE, STAMFORD
Taken by Cromwell at the start of the war. He presented a portrait of himself to the owner, the Countess of Exeter.

THE BATTLEFIELDS OF EDGEHILL, WARWICKSHIRE, MARSTON MOOR IN YORKSHIRE AND NASEBY IN NORTHAMPTONSHIRE
These are all marked by monuments.

THE BANQUETING HALL IN WHITEHALL
You can still see the window where Charles I stepped out to be executed.

OXBURGH HALL, NORFOLK
Many National Trust properties used to belong to families whose ancestors fought in the Civil War. One of these is Oxburgh Hall, where there is a collection of arms and armour from the time of the Civil War in the armoury.